Commitment

Commitment

Fatherhood in Black America

Artistic Concept and Photographs by
Carole Patterson

Guest Photographs by
Anthony Barboza

Essays by
Arvarh E. Strickland and Minion KC Morrison

Captions and Biographical Narratives by
Clyde Ruffin

Edited by
Marlene Perchinske
Museum of Art and Archaeology
University of Missouri–Columbia

University of Missouri Press
Columbia and London

Text copyright © 1998
by The Curators of the University of Missouri
Photographs copyright © 1998
by Carole Patterson and Anthony Barboza
University of Missouri Press, Columbia, Missouri 65201
Printed and bound in Italy

5 4 3 2 1   02 01 00 99 98

Library of Congress Cataloging-in-Publication Data

Patterson, Carole.
    Commitment : fatherhood in Black America / artistic
concept and photographs by Carole Patterson ; guest
photographs by Anthony Barboza ; essays by Arvarh E.
Strickland and Minion KC Morrison ; captions and
biographical narratives by Clyde Ruffin ; edited by
Marlene Perchinske.
        p.   cm.
    ISBN: 0-8262-1157-7 (alk. paper)
    1. Afro-American fathers—Psychology. 2. Afro-
American fathers—Attitudes. 3. Afro-American
fathers—Social conditions. 4. Afro-American families—
Social conditions. I. Ruffin, Clyde. II. Barboza, Anthony,
1944–. III. Title.
    HQ756.P393   1998
    306.874'2 21
                                                97-22908
                                                CIP

∞   This paper meets the requirements of the
American National Standard for Permanence of Paper
for Printed Library Materials, Z39.48, 1984.

Design and composition: Kristie Lee
Printer and binder: Milanostampa USA Inc.
Typefaces: Avant Garde and Berkeley

The photographs on pages 58, 61, 74, 77, 79, 81, 82,
and 85 are by Anthony Barboza.

I dedicate my work, with love, to my father, W. R. Cheek, and to all fathers who generously commit themselves to their families.

—Carole Patterson

Contents

Editor's Acknowledgments

This publication documents the exhibition *Commitment: Fatherhood in Black America*, which opened at the Museum of Art and Archaeology, University of Missouri–Columbia, on October 18, 1997, and closed on December 14, 1997. The exhibition consists of fifty black-and-white photographs that depict twelve devoted fathers and their families. The idea for the exhibition and this publication was conceived and orchestrated with admirable passion by photographer Carole Patterson. Together, her photographs and personal commitment bring the subject of fatherhood in black America to the forefront of discussion in contemporary society, countering the negative images of fatherhood in black America that are so prevalent. We owe Carole immense gratitude for undertaking this important project, which brings to the public's attention fathers who have dedicated themselves to supporting and nurturing their children. A thank-you must also be extended to guest photographer Anthony Barboza for his contributions.

Initially, Anthony Radich, Director of the Missouri Arts Council, and Morteza Sajadian, Director of the Museum of Art and Archaeology, assisted. Both have since left their positions, as has Curator Christine Neal, who carried the project through its intermediate stages. A Missouri Arts Council grant and support from Minion KC Morrison, as Vice Provost for Minority Affairs at the University of Missouri, also provided assistance.

Early on, an advisory committee was formed. On April 16, 1994, the group met at the St. Louis Art Museum to discuss the exhibition and its publication.

Those involved and to whom we owe thanks are: Professor James Cone, Union Theological Seminary, N.Y.; Director Gerald Early, Department of African-American Studies, Washington University; and Curator Jackie Lewis Harris, St. Louis Art Museum. Special thanks must go to Arvarh Strickland, Minion KC Morrison, and Clyde Ruffin for their significant literary efforts.

Museum staff deserve additional credit for their teamwork—especially Owen Koeppe, the museum's interim director. Many thanks to Laura Wilson for bringing continuity to the project. Tremendous work on the part of Debra Page brought this project to completion with assistance from Luann Andrews, Jane Biers, Beth Cobb, Judi Dawson, Keith Fletcher, Debbie Friedrich, Scherrie Goettsch, David Gold, Jon Lawrence, Aimée Leonhard, Stacia Schaefer, Jacqueline Schneider, Brad Steinmetz, Greig Thompson, Bette Weiss, and Jeff Wilcox.

More thanks go to Elizabeth Revington Burdick for her enormous effort and dedication to the project. Contributions were also made by Minority Men's Network and Monica Naylor.

Without the patience and expert advice of Director Beverly Jarrett, Managing Editor Jane Lago, Designer Kristie Lee, and Production Manager Dwight Browne, all at the University of Missouri Press, this publication would not have been completed. Finally—and most important—we are indebted to the fathers who are found in these pages. Their contributions give an inner peace and strength to their children that benefit all humankind.

Marlene Perchinske

Photographer's Acknowledgments

I would like to express my heartfelt gratitude to family, friends, and associates who have given support and believed in me and my work.

To Marlene Perchinske, Director of the Museum of Art and Archaeology, for her commitment to guiding this book and exhibition to completion, I will always be grateful. For their initial encouragement and support, I am indebted to Anthony Radich and Morteza Sajadian and to the Missouri Arts Council.

A special thanks to Clyde Ruffin, who listened from the beginning and who then gathered the narratives so beautifully.

For their invaluable friendship and curatorial insight, thank you to Elizabeth Revington Burdick and Carol Bates, who gave freely of their time and energy.

For photographic assistance, my sincere thanks to Wesley Crain, Susan Dunkerley, Robert Simms, Peter Anger, and Deborah Bailey.

I appreciate the enthusiasm and support of Minion KC Morrison; Christine Neal; David Bradley; the Atlantic Center for the Arts; and Dale H. Creach, President of MFA Oil Company. I am grateful to the late Emmett Peter for introducing me to John Henry Moore, with whom I began this project.

For their continuing interest and enthusiasm, my thank-you to Susan Ailor, Father Greg Boyle, Kenneth L. Carl, James H. Cone, Barbara Azar Davis, Sylvan and Jane Dove, Lea Evans, Natalie Fitzgerald, Milton McC and Ione Gatch, Jon Lawrence, Jackie Lewis-Harris, Debra Page, Gerald and Marion Perkoff, James and Vera Olson, Margaret Sayers Peden, Ronald Ross, and Greig Thompson.

A special thank-you to Kathy Jacobsen and Janice Wendt of Satter, a division of Omega, for their contribution of paper on which the images for this book and exhibition have been printed.

My parents, W. R. and Lillian Cheek, my sister, Sharon Crain, and my daughter, Kimberly Pace, deserve special thanks for their love and support throughout my career.

Finally, I owe a special tribute to each of the fathers presented in this book. May their commitment and dedication provide yet another link among fathers and families of all races.

Carole Patterson

Commitment

Learning through History

Arvarh E. Strickland

Portraits of African American men as caring, nurturing fathers do not conform to the stereotypical family roles traditionally assigned to them. From treatments of the African American families by proslavery scholars to the Moynihan Report, black families have been characterized as dysfunctional, and the absence of a father has been used to explain the instability of the black family. Only in recent years have the positive, adaptive features of the black family been explored and the black father's place in his family been found to be more positive.

Studies of the black family have not yet come of age. For decades, studies of the African American family did not progress far beyond the negative conclusions reached by historian and slavery apologist Ulrich B. Phillips. Phillips maintained that African slaves brought only primitive cultural institutions with them to the Americas. The plantation became a school where Africans learned the European culture of the slave owners. "Eventually," Phillips wrote, "it could be said that the Negroes had no memories of Africa as a home." The black family, then, was a creation of slave owners. "The plantation was a matrimonial bureau, something of a harem perhaps, a copious nursery, and a divorce court."[1]

Phillips acknowledged that family structure varied among slaves. There were monogamous marriages, but most slave families were assumed to be matriarchal in structure. Some slave women and men were used to breed children for the profit of the owner. The assumed absence of slave fathers in most families and the use of male slaves in breeding fostered the stereotype of the black male as a profligate "stud." Phillips also acknowledged the exploitation of slave women by planters and their sons in concubinage arrangements.[2] Whatever the structure of the slave family, it was an unstable unit. For the family existed at the pleasure of the slave owner. Husbands and wives could be separated by sale or at the whim of the owner, and children could be sold away from their parents.

Edward Franklin Frazier, the pioneering African American sociologist and student of the black family, reached many of the same conclusions as Phillips.

Frazier's position was in keeping with his training by Robert E. Park, Ernest W. Burgess, Ellsworth Faris, and other members of the Chicago school of sociologists. Like Phillips, Frazier concluded that African Americans retained no African cultural heritage, and he agreed that the unstable black family was merely an imperfect copy of the white family.[3]

In both his study of the African American family in Chicago and his broader study of the black family in the United States, Frazier rejected the contention that the demoralization of black family life could be explained by the retention of African cultural traits. Instead, he posited the position that slavery destroyed the family as an African cultural institution. In its place, under slavery, an African American family system began to develop. In fact, according to Frazier, a degree of stability began to develop in this imitative system. This developing stability was disrupted, however, when emancipation broke the constraints exercised by the slave system.

The black family became further demoralized when rural blacks left agricultural regions and migrated to urban areas. Urbanization, Frazier contended, led to widespread desertion of their families by black men. Although Frazier was aware of the connection between poverty and family instability, he maintained that stable, middle-class families resulted largely from the close association of this group of African Americans, both in slavery and in freedom, with white Americans. In summarizing this point of view, he wrote:

> When one views in retrospect the waste of human life, the immorality, delinquency, desertion, and broken homes which have been involved in the development of Negro family life in the United States, they appear to have been the inevitable consequences of the attempt of a preliterate people, stripped of their cultural heritage, to adjust themselves to civilization. The very fact that the Negro has succeeded in adopting habits of living that have enabled him to survive in a civilization based upon laissez faire and competition, itself bespeaks a degree of success in taking on the folkways and mores of the master race.[4]

Frazier's works appeared during the years 1930–1940, a period that Andrew Billingsley called the "golden age for studies of Negro life." These were years when there was no war to be analyzed and the nation was undergoing the crisis of the Great Depression. Scholars turned their attention to studying ways of remedying the ills of society, and, this time, the African American was not neglected. By this time, an impressive group of African American scholars had joined the white scholars who were engaged in researching and writing about African American life.[5] For several decades, however, Frazier's conclusions about the nature of the black family were accepted as common wisdom.

The release of the Moynihan Report in 1965 caused the common wisdom to be questioned and brought renewed and more objective scholarly attention to studies of black families. This report, which was largely a political treatise, concluded that the fabric of African American society is deteriorating, and basic to this condition is the deterioration of the black family. The report cited as evidence of this deterioration the high divorce rate among African Americans and the large number of illegitimate births, which resulted in a high percentage of families headed by females.[6]

Daniel Moynihan drew upon the common wisdom as formulated by Frazier and elaborated upon by other scholars—including Nathan Glazer, Kenneth Clark, and Stanley M. Elkins. He characterized the black family as mired in a "tangle of pathology." A key element in this "pathology" was the status of the black male. "In essence," he said, "the Negro community has been forced into a matriarchal structure which, because it is so out of line with the rest of the American society, seriously retards the progress of the group as a whole, and imposes a crushing burden on the Negro male and, in consequence, on a great many Negro women as well."[7] Because African American men occupy a marginal position in the economy, they are unable to perform the roles of strong husbands and fathers. Children reared in broken homes are not prepared to compete in society. They drop out of school, are unable to qualify for employment, and become a part of a cycle of poverty. Consequently, Moynihan concluded that governmental policy must be directed toward bringing stability to the black family.

A major contribution of the Moynihan Report was the controversy it raised and the impetus it brought to renewed scholarly studies of the black family. John Blassingame and other scholars turned to African

American sources and came away with a radically different view of African American life under slavery and during the first years of freedom. These scholars found that an African American culture developed in the slave quarters based upon both African heritage and Euro-American elements. The family, as adapted in the culture of the quarters, played an important role in the acculturation of slave children. Moreover, although the slave father's authority was limited and he could not perform the crucial role of protecting his family, he played significant roles in the lives of his wife and children.[8] Leon F. Litwack, in his prizewinning study of the transition of African Americans from slavery to freedom, did not find the former slaves' lives to be characterized by pathology. "If the ex-slaves were to succeed," he wrote, "they would have to depend largely on their own resources." He continued: "Under these constraints, a recently enslaved people sought ways to give meaning to their new status. The struggles they would be forced to wage to shape their lives and destinies as free men and women remain to this day an epic chapter in the history of the American people."[9]

The most thorough revisionist study of the black family inspired by the Moynihan Report was that made by Herbert G. Gutman. Through exhaustive research in state and federal census data, Freedmen's Bureau records, manuscript collections, and other sources, Gutman provided convincing evidence that slavery did not produce a fatherless matrifocal family structure that was handed down from generation to generation, even into the last half of the twentieth century. He also showed that the absence of fathers was not the dominant characteristic of urban African American households in 1855 and 1875 and in 1905 and 1925. Through careful analysis of naming practices among African American families, Gutman demonstrated that black families in slavery and freedom developed meaningful family relationships and passed this institutional structure from generation to generation.[10]

The fact remains, however, that the African American family has serious problems. In 1992, Andrew Hacker pointed to the disturbing statistics that confirm this problem. "Nearly two thirds of black babies are now born outside of wedlock, and over half of black families are headed by women. The majority of black youngsters live only with their mother; and in over half of these households, she has never been married." Still, Hacker cautioned against hasty generalizations and invidious comparisons of white and black families. A careful analysis revealed that there is now a trend toward homes headed by mothers both in the United States and throughout the world. Moreover, this trend began fairly recently. In 1950, both fathers and mothers were present in over 80 percent of black homes and in over 90 percent of white homes. Poverty and welfare dependence are major concerns expressed about the absence of black fathers. There is also the concern that the lack of a father figure may contribute to the delinquency of teenage male youth.[11]

Hacker and other scholars now point out that poverty is a major determinant of family stability. Moreover, poverty is not just an African American phenomenon in our society. According to a 1978 census report, for both blacks and whites, the proportion of children living with both parents appeared to be related to family income. In 1975, in black families with incomes under $4,000, only 20 percent of the children lived with both parents, but in families with incomes at or over $15,000, 86 percent of black children were living with both a mother and a father. In the 1980s, a majority of both white and black families with income below the poverty level were single-parent or single-person households. Over three-fourths of households with income above $25,000 were husband-wife families.

Nevertheless, poverty has been most devastating to the black family. But the problem facing the African American family is not poverty alone. According to psychiatrists William H. Grier and Price M. Cobbs, the primary cause of the weakness of the black family is the institutional structure of the nation that keeps the black family from protecting its members. If the black family is to be strengthened, they maintain, there must be a "change in the fabric of the nation" so that a black man can "extend physical protection to his family everywhere, throughout the country." While others have seen the weaknesses and not the strengths of the African American family, the much maligned black man "has found sufficient nourishment to endure and bring forth issue, to exploit his strengths, and to relentlessly attack the social order which limits the expanse of his most precious place."[12]

It is interesting that Herbert Gutman considered a photograph to be the most telling source in his magnificent study. He said, "The most important single piece of historical evidence in this book is neither an isolated statistic, a historical 'anecdote,' a numerical table, nor a chart. It is the photograph that adorns the jacket of this book and serves as its frontispiece." This picture of eight African American men, women, and children is entitled "Five generations on Smith's plantation, Beaufort, South Carolina."[13]

Without the more than six hundred pages of text that comprise Gutman's book, the people depicted in *Commitment: Fatherhood in Black America* carry a strong message about African American families. The portraits of fathers, children, and families are both art and text. In many ways, they are as moving to the viewer as are masterpieces of art, but they also carry a message. Young fathers, older fathers, a great-grandfather, fathers on different levels of the economic ladder give the portraits universal scope. At this time, when emphasis is being placed on making it possible for young African American men to fulfill their roles as husbands and fathers, these portraits are an excellent medium for carrying a message to young people about the obligations and responsibilities of parenthood. We learn from history that this message is timeless because it has been an enduring part of the African American experience.

1. Ulrich Bonnell Phillips, *Life and Labor in the Old South* (Boston and Toronto: Little, Brown and Co., 1929, 1957, 1963), 194-96.

2. Ibid., 203-5.

3. The discussion of Frazier's work is based on his three books on black family life: *The Negro Family in Chicago* (Chicago: University of Chicago Press, 1932); *The Free Negro Family: A Study of Family Origins before the Civil War* (Nashville: Fisk University Press, 1932), and *The Negro Family in the United States* (Chicago: University of Chicago Press, 1939).

4. Frazier, *The Negro Family in the United States,* 487.

5. Andrew Billingsley, *Black Families in White America* (Englewood Cliffs, N.J.: Prentice Hall, 1968), 204-5.

6. Daniel Moynihan, *The Negro Family: The Case for National Action* (Washington, D.C.: Office of Policy Planning and Research, U.S. Department of Labor, 1965).

7. Lee Rainwater and William L. Yancey, *The Moynihan Report and the Politics of Controversy* (Cambridge, Mass., and London: MIT Press, 1967), 75.

8. See, for example, John W. Blassingame, *The Slave Community: Plantation Life in the Antebellum South,* rev. ed. (New York and Oxford: Oxford University Press, 1979), chap. 4.

9. Leon F. Litwack, *Been in the Storm So Long: The Aftermath of Slavery* (New York: Alfred A. Knopf, 1979), xiv.

10. See Herbert G. Gutman, *The Black Family in Slavery and Freedom, 1750-1925* (New York: Pantheon, 1976, 1977).

11. Andrew Hacker, *Two Nations: Black and White, Separate, Hostile, Unequal* (New York: Charles Scribner's Sons, 1992), chap. 5.

12. William H. Grier and Price M. Cobbs, *Black Rage* (New York: Basic Books, 1968) chap. 5, quotations on pp. 84 and 101.

13. Gutman, *The Black Family,* xxiv.

Learning through Memory

Minion KC Morrison

Core black culture is more than ad hoc synchronic adaptive survival. Its values, systems of logic and world view are rooted in a lengthy peasant tradition and clandestine theology. It is the notion of sacrifice for kin, the belief in the natural sequence of cause and effect—"Don't nothin' go over the devil's back but don't bind him under the belly." It is a classical, restricted notion of the possible. It esteems the deed more than the wish, venerates the 'natural man' over the sounding brass of machine technology and has the wit to know that "Everybody talking 'bout Heaven ain't going there."[1]

I

Perhaps in thinking of one's father one always begins at the beginning   exploring the delicacy of his hand, the steadiness of his gait, his larger-than-life presence. It is there that we as sons get our bearings for our own sense of delicacy, our gaits, and the weight of the world as it envelops and defines our "daddy." Some of this weight and enveloping is common stuff   the working, the providing that men do. Other parts are more complex—men's relationships with their peers, with their women (wives, lovers, friends). Others are deep, enduring and jaundiced—being black and poor, or rich and professional, or blue collar. Some are mood things—gray, blue, the red of temper, the subtle texture and mixture of colors swirling in the wide expanse of a father's laughter. Like a rare perfect thing, these fleeting moments of delicacy with daddy present themselves. The moments provide a context for the occasional silence, the distance, and the all-consuming nature of work that makes them inaccessible too often. But oh, the marvel when we are wrapped so tightly around them that their gaits become our gaits, their laughter ours, and more!

Yet for some of us—black and poor or rich, so trapped by what ought to be and by the longing most of us have to be just ordinary black folk—these delicate moments that define us as boys, men, fathers, friends are truncated, nonexistent. When it is too much to be black and whatever else—we run, take

wild escapades to disaster; or we are snatched, ensnared into a system designed to destroy all opportunities for rapture with our children, wives, lovers, friends, colleagues; and sometimes we lose all knowledge of who we are and the ability to love ourselves. We are the jobless, imprisoned, homeless lot—often in a drug-induced surreal fog, seeking a reality and peace of mind and body where there is none. And so we are absent—gone from ourselves and from any sense of family or fatherhood.

Despite this trauma, what we offer here are fathers who have assumed all the roles to inspire rapture in sons and daughters and family. Like Maya Angelou's sisters rising, these men rise to assume places and spaces in the lives of their children and families. These photographs bring us the men whose existence is so often denied or rendered ambiguous because others are privileged to make African American representations.

Who are the fathers who provide the tradition-giving context and moment to this exhibition and catalog? How may we know them? Are they not so precious few that rendering them absent or ambiguous may be just as well? It is our assertion that there have always been these fathers to be watched, and to serve as mentors in the family writ large. Indeed they have always been available to us in the sort of African-inspired extended families we all used to relish. While this family extension was not as complicated as that organized in West African societies, for example, it had a definite structure and was laden with expectations and consequences. It provided a plethora of men to be observed and emulated and from whom a way of seeing the world could be acquired.

At the point of its greatest prominence, family extension allowed grandparents, uncles, aunts, cousins, and surrogates thereof to make obligatory claims upon their peers and children. There were deep personal relationships in the close residential quarters relatives and other members of the community occupied. Families helped each other in maintaining a livelihood and shared responsibilities for raising children. Young children were often raised by grandparents or uncles and aunts, and they shared sibling-type relationships with cousins. These communal parents had all the rights to socialize, exact punishment, and issue instructions for members of such a local community.[2]

This communal system historically provided license for members to lay claim to all prominent African Americans as fathers, geographic location and basis for leadership notwithstanding. By these rules prominent black figures in the local community and beyond belonged to the entire black community. In part the common experience of living in a system where racism operated essentially as public policy helped to sustain this communal understanding. And so, Nat Turner, while not well known among the white community, is widely known and appropriated as a symbol and as an imposing arbiter—father and brother—among black men. Similarly, Adam Clayton Powell was not just a congressman from Harlem; the whole black world owned and had expectations of him. These men as fathers, brothers, and sons provided models for all of us similarly affected by racial caste.

This license gives to the black community a wide range of other fathers for appropriation, providing all the roles and expectations that male figures commonly serve in socially organized settings. They are in every sense providers, role models, and sustainers of a body of traditions of substance, value, and desirability. They are assigned status on the strength of what John Gwaltney has called core black culture. "[F]ar more often than not, the primary status of a black person is that accorded by the people he or she lives among. It is based upon assessments of that person's fidelity to core black standards." These assignations are made, he argues, because "[t]heir feelings of personal and communal satisfaction are rooted in the astonishing reality of their civil, principled survival in spite of the weight of empire that rests upon their backs."[3]

Some of them are nameless, known only in their local places. I have seen them as I was doing fieldwork in urban and rural places all over the United States, living and functioning as a grounded member of black communities. I conjure them sitting on "lazy benches" in southern towns; on deacon boards in churches; around barbecue pits; "woofing and lying" in bars and barbershops; holding their baby girls and patting their growing sons atop their heads—dubbing them "little lady" and "lil' man."

They are available too in our written history so lavishly rendered by Carter G. Woodson and John Hope Franklin, and sometimes in their own words— Frederick Douglass, David Walker, W. E. B. Du Bois,

Martin Luther King. They also people the laments of Langston Hughes, the anger of Richard Wright, the longings of Margaret Walker. They wrestle around inside themselves in the works of Ralph Ellison and offer their visions with such rapture and grace in those of Toni Morrison.

The history of black men in the United States, at least when we are looking at ourselves, presents a picture of fatherhood and familyhood clear back to chattel slavery, a system designed to destroy all vestiges of personal independence and responsibility. Yet here existed men and women under the worst possible circumstances creating communities and long-term family unions. They were not generally doing so under the color of law and maintained these unions almost always under the threat of disruption. John Blassingame suggests these independent "slave communities" resulted because "[t]he social organization of the quarters was the slave's primary environment which gave him ethical rules and fostered cooperation, mutual assistance, and black solidarity." A distinct culture was thus created—"an emotional religion, folk songs and tales, dances and superstitions . . . language, customs, beliefs, and ceremonies." Indeed:

> Having a distinct culture helped the slaves to develop a strong sense of group solidarity. They united to protect themselves from the most oppressive features of slavery and to preserve their self-esteem. Despite their weakness as isolated individuals, they found some protection in the group from their masters. The code of the group, for example, called for support of these slaves who broke plantation rules. The most important aspect of this group identification was that slaves were not solely dependent on the white man's cultural frames of reference for their ideals and values. As long as the plantation black had cultural norms and ideals, ways of verbalizing aggression, and roles in his life largely free from his master's control, he could preserve some personal autonomy, and resist infantilization, total identification with planters, and internalization of unflattering stereotypes calling for abject servility.[4]

And there were families too. Contrary to the popular myths, blacks maintained a huge number of sustained monogamous relationships under the dire circumstances of slavery. Herbert Gutman, looking at plantation records, has documented these families— defined as a man, a woman, and their children. Studying records from around the end of enslavement, he found a majority of the adults in double-headed units of considerable duration. In several Virginia counties alone between 1865 and 1866 more than 76 percent of those formerly enslaved lived in double-headed families, the bulk with children present. And in another set of counties some 53 percent of these units had endured for more than ten years, and nearly 20 percent of them for twenty years or more.[5] The data are similar for North Carolina, Mississippi, Louisiana, Tennessee, and Kentucky.

II

Of course, those of us who have black fathers, and have grown with them and been privileged to watch or be mentored by them, wonder at the prolonged myth of their absence and negligence. For us they have always been there as our blood fathers, or as a part of the extended family. We know them as our providers and nurturers, as men who were products of their socialization in a male-dominated world, bearing that special susceptibility for blame and victimization in a racist society. But that was given — it was a part of the baggage of us all. Our fathers showed us paths for resistance and success nevertheless.

I look back on my own case, having lost a father to a natural death at six years of age. But there is this presence in the spare memories I have. There was a setting in snow—likely the first I ever saw, as it comes to me now so vividly white. There were also birds— red birds and blue birds, being trapped by this perpetual hunting man. Yet I do not remember a single bird dying. Or that other time when I was thrown up on one of his horses—a big thing I could have no hope of controlling. And here I was pulling at its leather strapping, trying to make it go. I was fearless. My daddy made this world all so small for me. And how he loved and doted on my sister too—making her everybody's little queen.

And Grandpapa, I possessed him longer! How consummately I possessed him, too—watching him smoke his pipe with such authority, letting the smoke encircle his entirely white pate with such regal confidence. And then his quiet way—assigning me nothing, but allowing me to take what I willed or had no choice but to take.

And then the other fathers at church, at school, in the street. All in a place so small that one could not help but know them all; their foibles and virtues. But

this access gave me a world of delicate moments to wake and sleep to, defining all, as I appropriated a model here and there, understanding and growing into my own gait and laughter and way of communicating. But perhaps more than anything else, I had absolute certainty and integrity in the black boy I was as I grew up comfortably grounded in a culture, the understanding of which gave me an ability to wallow in its folkways, and to assume all its risks in a racist society.

These stories of fathers and sons are so rarely told for their ordinariness. And those that are told are more rarely still accessible in that space where things become defining. They are stories that happen in our private interactions, or their literary renderings are the stuff of legend among specialists. But they exist and, like the photographs in this exhibition and catalog, flesh out the story that we have always known of the marvel of these fathers across generations in the United States.

They include John Edgar Wideman's description of that trip he waited too long to take with his father to a place called "promised land," and then his efforts to make his own son understand the story and its meaning.

> I know my father's name, Edgar, and some of his father's names, *Hannibal, Tatum, Jordan*, but I can't go back any further than a certain point, except I also know the name of a place, Greenwood, South Carolina, and an even smaller community, Promised Land, nearly abutting Greenwood, where my grandfather, who's of course your great-grandfather, was born, and many of his brothers are buried there under sturdy tombstones, bearing his name, our name, *Wideman* carved in stone in the place where the origins of the family begin to dissolve into the loam of plantations owned by white men, where my grandfathers' identities dissolve, where they were boys, then men, and the men they were fade into a set of facts, sparse, ambiguous, impersonal, their intimate lives unretrievable, where what is known about a county, a region, a country and its practice of human bondage, its tradition of obscuring, stealing, or distorting black people's lives, begins to crowd out the possibility of seeing my ancestors as human beings. The powers and principalities that originally restricted our access to the life free people naturally enjoy still rise like a shadow, a wall between my grandfathers and myself, my father and me, between the two of us, father and son, son and father.[6]

There is also the well-wrought life of Joe Young-blood in John Oliver Killens's story of a black family in Crossroads, Georgia, making the transition from slavery. The members of this family are the working poor, but they are so confident in themselves. Despite the vulnerability of Youngblood in the mill where he works and is subjected to abuse and violence, and in circumstances where he is unable to protect his wife and children, he and they are rendered whole. They eke out a living and a way of being—their culture and creativity operating therein are ubiquitous and solid. They move about from their two-room shack to a core community of others—teachers, preachers, neighbors, workers—living under the same strains and with the same foibles and virtues. They are all pushing the horizons of their special limits in wise ways, but ultimately insisting on integrity, even when it means death.[7]

The fathers of whom I speak are rendered not only via literary devices. They include the real lived examples in our own time of Daddy King and his sons and daughters, one Martin having earned so much fame. More often they are fathers like the postal workers in Noel Casenave's study who perceived themselves to be much more engaged with their growing children than had been their fathers before, changing diapers and all the rest of it. They were working, but they were not "work machines or work addicts." These fathers saw work as "a means to an end . . . providing, and providing itself is seen as a means to effectively carry out the husband and father roles."[8]

Or they are those fathers in the "Million Man March," making a public statement of their willingness to move beyond the limits of public myth—a march with fathers, brothers, and sons, or would-be fathers and would-be sons—generations of men trying to learn to deal with each other. Anonymous often, drawn together by the common experience of living in a colonial-like state, burdened with racial myths and a fractured identity perpetrated by others, they are memorialized in *Get on the Bus*, Spike Lee's cinematic version, which uses the march as mere backdrop for eavesdropping on the musings and struggles of fathers, brothers, and sons with each other.

Or, they are this anonymous character:

> Walking through the streets of Boston with my father always felt like being at the center of a parade. Dad would strut like Black royalty . . .

I ambled along next to him, my soft, little beige hand wrapped around two or three of his thick golden fingers. . . . Before long our float would stop and he would plant his feet shoulder-width apart, hands on his hips. . . . He stood still and strong while he conversed, never shifting his feet. He could be animated and passionate, but his movement remained focused and sharp. And so, it seemed did he. His physical presence conveyed a control of himself, and by extension, the conversation. It seemed that he was in control of the world around him.[9]

III

To be sure there were other men about us who possessed none of the requisites. But neither were they fathers to us; they occupied other roles. Some were the social misfits found in any community. Far too many were casualties of an enslaved and colonized condition, impotent and trapped by an omnipresent, grinding racism. We have never been prepared to accept that it was they who defined us as men, as fathers, and as family providers. But define us they have.

> Always more to us than meets the eye. Our eyes or the eyes of others who don't want to know what the more might be, who expend a lot of energy pretending there isn't more, insisting there must not be more. We carry the burden, the responsibility, the challenge and joy of creating the little extra, the something more that keeps us not exactly what we're supposed to be. What the novelist Richard Wright called a battle between blacks and whites over the nature of reality begins here, where we make up ourselves and share with those others who would love us. If we're different, who decides the meaning of that difference? Who shall create its form and who shall benefit from it?
>
> The person like me because we are both different is sharing the work of giving meaning to difference. The ones who appear like us, whom we meet in the street, are other answers-in-progress coping for better or worse with the puzzle of our identity. Although we can pretend not to, we see ourselves in them. How do we sustain within ourselves the determination, grit, the voice saying yes, we can do it, yes. Not only am I surviving, out here doing, as you see, my thing but there's more, more to me, and I'm doing that work too. Being me, not what difference makes of me.[10]

This is really about image making and the creation of identity. Despite a long tradition of blacks confidently defining themselves in the places where they operated with a degree of independence, this possession has been less than complete. Hence the struggle that Wideman portrays is a constant. "American culture" insofar as such exists is rarely defined in terms of its African referents, let alone with any primacy assigned to them. At its least the society sees itself as a Western, European culture. The understanding of Africans in juxtaposition to Europe was long since established to be "danger versus purity," "depraved versus civilized."[11] This allowed for chattel slavery, overlaid with capitalism, which continues to thrive on the manipulation of black labor.

In large measure this racist conceptualization of African Americans and the manipulation of their labor sustain practices that define black people, and fathers in particular, as negative figures. They are portrayed stereotypically, bound up in myths of violence, depravity, psychosexual fantasy; they are seen as unemployed sloths alienated from or unresponsive to their women and children. These myths and fantasies are themselves fulfilling prophesies, sustained with the statistics of paternal absence, criminality, and unemployment—mistaking consequence for cause.

The negative images assigned to the community have been exceedingly effective throughout history. Winthrop Jordan has documented this from Plato's notions of the "chain of being" to Aristotle and Thomas Jefferson's assertions of African inferiority. And Rhett Jones has surveyed the science of this image making, illustrating everything from psychosocial interpretation to brain size as definitive of black inferiority.[12]

Some of the most complex parts of this imaging remain the visual representations of depravity, lust, ignorance, and body caricatures. Blacks have been seen as near-people, dumb little "black Sambos" fawning for favor, and studs preoccupied with sex. These fantasies, of course, have created their own self-fulfilling prophesies of a sexual-performance competition and the presumed covetousness of black men for "virtuous" white women. The frequent association of lynchings with presumed or contrived violations of racial sex taboos is revealing. And in our own time the horror of the lynching of Emmett Till for supposedly whistling at a white woman stands boldly symbolic.

This is especially true in contemporary times with the rapidity and range with which the images are disseminated. Witness Willie Horton as a symbol of "criminalized" black males, sustained by statistics showing their greater incarceration even in places like Wyoming, where blacks hardly live. In this context Kobina Mercer suggests that "black masculinity is not merely a social identity in crisis, it is also a key site of ideological representation, a site upon which the nation's crisis comes to be dramatized, demonized, and dealt with."[13]

No less complex is what Bell Hooks calls the "commodification of blackness" that allows the "feminization" of the black male body in commerce. She argues that this process converts what would be an image of strength, if used for some political end, to one of weakness. The definition of the image remains external to the black community. "The quintessential symbol of the fetishized eroticized black male body as object of spectacle is the image of Michael Jordan" speaking "to the cartoon figure of Bugs Bunny as though they are equals."[14]

IV

This exhibition and catalog accept the challenge of presenting images built around the ordinary way the community "carries itself" when expressing independence. These artists do not seek to divorce these fathers from context. For it is within a context that they become real, especially in a situation where "the face of white supremacy has not changed over time, . . . [so] that the end of representation remains a crucial realm of struggle, perhaps even more important than the question of equal access."[15] These artists have sought to capture and reveal fathers, whatever their personal situations, as they play out their roles as providers and nurturers. Photographer Carole Patterson suggests something of this view in describing the way she composes:

> I have attempted to photograph the relationships within these families by engaging them in conversation, learning what they do, watching them in their daily lives. I see something that looks good through the lens—and I have to watch them through the camera a lot of the time. Then I seize the moment—capture their spirit, so to speak. That's when it's like magic

to me. I see what's natural for them, and that's what I capture. These images then become their moments.[16]

Anthony Barboza suggests the same thing when he says, "I always worked on photos of people in the streets. Really, I come from a photojournalistic background in that sense." For him pictures have always been larger than just the representation on paper. They are stories of people's lives and circumstances. Barboza refers to these stories as his real education. He says, "Photography allows me to meet people. And one can learn more from people than one can learn from books or anything else."[17]

The aim is to represent the range of roles assumed by black fathers—at church, at work, at play; performing personal-care responsibilities; doting on their children and vice versa; and forever offering a model for babies, adolescents, and young adults. The images show fathers and sons, fathers and daughters, and the family. They are not meant to symbolize the full range of possibilities in the African American community. The focus is on fathers. Fathers who in their ordinariness as blacks are largely lost from view, as much by intention as otherwise. They are those said not to exist, not recognized for the tremendous responsibilities they carry in raising their children, supporting their families, and helping sustain their communities.

Carole Patterson's description of how she came to do the project is consistent with these efforts to alter the stereotypically negative ways in which black males are portrayed in society. The concern is broad, but it happens that her medium is photography; she describes how she came to see her work as a means of contributing to image building, allowing the principals to speak for themselves. She details how the vision began to be shaped by that horrifying image of the Emmett Till lynching.

> One of the three or four most earthshaking public events in my life—I can't talk about it without having tears in my eyes—was, as a young girl, hearing about the death of Emmett Till. My mother came in and as she read the newspaper story about it we wept. Why? This little boy was killed! Simply because of the color of his skin, he had suffered this fate. I was so upset that I didn't go to school that day. And that memory has hung on my shoulder as if it happened yesterday.

James Baldwin, whom she eventually was to meet and photograph, made a deep impression on what she calls her "social consciousness." Many years later, she reread *Nobody Knows My Name* en route to pick up her daughter at a southern college.

> As we started home, I saw a man on the median of the highway on campus. I asked, "Kimberly, what is he passing out?" She said, "Mother, this is the South, and the Ku Klux Klan, as long as they're in a suit, can still hand out literature on Sundays on the highway on campus."
> Something just went through me like a bolt of lightning. I knew that I wanted to do something with my camera to promote better racial understanding. As I was visiting with a colleague, I said, "There is so much negative publicity about the black male. I watch very little television, but every time you turn it on, it's a negative image. Every time you open a newspaper there's a negative image. I'd like to concentrate on a different image from the media image of the African American male."

Anthony Barboza was invited by Carole Patterson to be a part of the project that she conceived. And he brought to it a career of photographing blacks in his community, among other things. What he brings as well, by obligation, is all the tutelage he received as the son of a black father who struggled but seemed to leave for his son a place to occupy as a black in American society with integrity. And the journey for this father was special, being the son of Cape Verdians in New Bedford, Massachusetts. But, Barboza says,

> Oh, my father did inspire me—he just always worked. He never gave up working. And God knows he never complained that much. But he complained. You remember the complaining. You remember that. You remember there is no money. You remember that. But my family was a unit of strength; so they were always together there. It always fits to be a family.

1. John Gwaltney, *Drylongso* (New York: Random House, 1980), xxvii.
2. See Robert Staples, *Introduction to Black Sociology* (New York: McGraw-Hill, 1976).
3. Gwaltney, *Drylongso*, xxiii, xxii.

4. John Blassingame, *The Slave Community: Plantation Life in the Antebellum South*, rev. ed. (New York: Oxford University Press, 1979), 105, 147–48.

5. Herbert Gutman, *The Black Family in Slavery and Freedom, 1750–1925* (New York: Pantheon, 1976), 11–12.

6. John Edgar Wideman, *Fatheralong: A Meditation on Fathers and Sons, Race and Society* (New York: Vintage, 1995), 196–97.

7. John Oliver Killens, *Youngblood* (Athens: University of Georgia Press, 1982).

8. Noel Casenave, "Middle-Income Black Fathers: An Analysis of the Provider Role," *Family Coordinator* 5.28, no. 4 (October 1979): 588.

9. Anonymous, "Finding My Stride," *Essence* 27.7 (November 1996): 102.

10. Wideman, *Fatheralong*, x–xi.

11. Winthrop Jordan, *White over Black: American Attitudes toward the Negro, 1550–1812* (New York: Norton, 1977), 19.

12. Ibid.; Rhett Jones, "Proving Blacks Inferior," in *The Death of White Sociology*, ed. Joyce Ladner (New York: Vintage, 1973), 114–35.

13. Mercer quoted in Thelma Golden, "My Brother," in *Black Male: Representations of Masculinity in Contemporary Art*, ed. Thelma Golden (New York: Whitney Museum, 1994), 19–43.

14. Bell Hooks, "Feminism Inside: Toward a Black Body Politic," in *Black Male*, ed. Golden, 134.

15. Julie Felner, Anastasia Higginbotham, and Bell Hooks, "Black (and White) Snapshots," *Ms* 5.2 (September 1994): 82-87.

16. Interview with Carole Patterson, Columbia, Mo., January 28, 1997.

17. Interview with Anthony Barboza, New York, November 1, 1996.

John Henry Moore

Born January 3, 1907, Effingham County, Georgia

"See this little bud the size of a safety pin here? You put it in a tree and wrap it tight with wax tape, and you take that off within three weeks. If it ain't took it'll turn brown and die, but if it's turned green, then it took. If it's green you take it and bury it and soon it'll come up, and in about three years it'll make a seedling, and from that seedling you'll get a tree fifty or sixty feet tall."

"There were ten boys in our family . . . ten boys. Sixty-five, seventy years ago, we didn't have no buses to ride. We were five miles from where they were teaching school and had to walk. We went to our little four- or five- or six-hour schooling, but when we come home every one of us had a job to do: scrubbing, sweeping, cutting big loads of wood, catching rabbits and catfish. Everybody planted gardens in those days: onions, peas, beans, okra, squash—and my mother always jarred up everything . . . fresh from the garden.

"They talk about bad times, but they don't know nothing about bad times. I worked hard, farming pumpkin, corn, peas, sweet potatoes, peaches, pears, apples . . . and at the end of the year the boss took it all. You could walk into a store and if a white couple was there talking, I don't care what you need, they didn't stop to wait on you. They finished their conversation and maybe they would turn around and say, 'Boy, what you want?' But my parents taught me that as long as a person don't put a hand on you, they can say anything they want to say. You take it because God said, 'Vengeance is mine!' That's what our forefathers taught us in the days gone by."

Frank Moore, a friend of John Henry Moore's, convinced him that he could have a better life in Florida than as a farmhand on a Georgia plantation. In the early months of 1926 Moore loaded up his few possessions and moved to Florida, where he found a job laying track for the railroad. He began to enjoy going from place to place and swore that it wasn't time for him to marry. In the fall of 1929 he met Rosa Lee

Norwood and changed his mind; the next year they were married.

"When my wife was during her best time, we went everywhere . . . most times twice a year. My parents took her in like one of the family. My mother loved her, my sister loved her, and my brothers. We'd take a bus into Jackson, not a Greyhound but the Florida Motorlines. We'd go up there and stay with them Christmas and the Fourth of July. Back in the old days there was love in the land, but love has taken a vacation."

Rosa Moore died in 1981. She and Moore had two sons. One died in infancy; the other, John Henry Jr., lived to the age of fifty. He died in 1983, the same year that Moore's great-grandson, Demetrius Antwan, was born. In 1987, at the age of eighty, Moore became the sole guardian of Demetrius, age four.

Moore rises every morning to prepare a breakfast of grits and eggs or oatmeal and is always home when Demetrius returns from school in the afternoon. They ride to the park to watch the ducks or spend quiet afternoons driving to visit an old friend at Furgee's fruit stand or to the fish market for crabs and shrimp. They take the tractor out once a week, just for fun, so that Moore "won't rust." Demetrius has a basketball goal outside the window where he can play in the dusty grass, never far away from Moore's cautious eye. There are always spiritual lessons and Sunday morning services with newly shined shoes, pressed suits, and long walks beneath the branches of the orange trees.

"I would like for the children to remember that back then I had to beg and plead, but I don't have to do that now. I learned to stand steady and see the power of God move. It was nothing but faith that gave me hope. Nothing else. We didn't have no other fighting means but prayer. Just prayer. God said if you go out and try to fight your battle and haven't considered me, I'll let the enemy kill you. But if you stand still, I'll fight your battle. You might lose your life but you have another life living in eternity."

"His mother, she was out there like many of the young people, just going place to place. So I taken Demetrius in and I'm still doing that today. I try to train him. I do the best I can. I pray. I'm doing everything I can to keep him in shape. He's going to have a hard time, but I try to tell him to do what's right. The scriptures tell you, 'Do unto men as you would have them do unto you.'"

Grandfathers and great-grandfathers
Their hands, strong and black, like leather
Thick jointed fingers clasped in humble submission
Proud voice rising
Rising deep from centuries of despair and neglect
Mighty men of peace
With strength to know that
There is power in the father's house.

"I worked for Mr. Emmet Peter for at least fifty years, as
a laborer in the grove, picking oranges by hand, fertilizing
by hand, and pulling moss off of trees by hand. Any time
a man can pick a hundred boxes a day, he was styled as a
number-one picker. Once, I did that for six straight days,
so I styled myself a 'good picker.' Back in those days we got
between six and ten cents a box, which was way more than
you could make doing day work where you worked ten
straight hours for a dollar a day."

"Oh, the pleasure that little boy has brought into my life;
I can't imagine what it would have been like without him
these past years."

Their lives are filled with familiar daily rituals through which Demetrius has inherited a vital legacy of strength and survival that transcends generations.

"For every child you have to thank God. There is nobody on God's earth that's going to be able to help America until this generation turns back to God. A mother and father's job is to raise a good son or a good daughter. The father needs to be in the home because when he speaks, there is something about the voice. He will be heard."

Gerald Russell

Born November 9, 1942, Little Rock, Arkansas

"Most of our family life is built around a family thing. Even now, every Friday all the kids and grandkids come over. I have a cookout, barbecue and fried fish—the whole thing. We sit out on the deck and find out what everybody's been doing over the week."

"I had a scholarship offer from just about all the colleges in the United States. I really wanted to go to the University of Arkansas and play for the Razorbacks, but they were not accepting any blacks. They even had an article in the paper that they were never going to have a black athlete up there. I was the first black high school all-American, but I made a mistake and took a trade class. I spent half a day on a trade and didn't apply myself to math, English, or anything like that. Recruiters wanted me to go to Los Angeles or Michigan, Colorado, Missouri, or Kansas. All that would have been fine, but I didn't have the classes to get in most of the colleges. They wanted me to go to a junior college for two years, but I thought I was too good of an athlete for that. It hurt. I didn't have nobody telling me which way to go, so I just dropped out.

"I came back home and my coach took me to the University of Tennessee. I was a sprinter in high school and they were looking for a big shoot-out in track. Wilma Rudolf was there, and they was looking forward to me entering this big race. But my wife got pregnant, and the way I was raised, if you plant a seed, then whatever you do, stand behind it. So I dropped out of college, come home, and got married. I never did go back. I just started working. That was thirty-four years ago."

Russell and his wife, Ollie, an elementary school teacher, were married in 1963. They have four children: Lauren, who is employed with Channel 11 in Little Rock; Gerald Jr., a respiratory therapist; Derek, a wide receiver with the Houston Oilers; and Felicia, a junior high school teacher.

"At times I have regrets, especially when I used to see people that I went to school with. But I kept moving on. A lot of my friends, they were going on to college and graduating. I look back sometimes and say I'm making more money than them, but I have to work a lot of long hours. I worked those long hours for so many years that now I ain't satisfied unless I'm working.

"A lot of evenings I come in after putting in twelve hours on my job, I get out there and wash three cars. I come back into the house and I might mop and wax the kitchen. Trying to raise a family and guide them to the right way of life, you don't have a whole lot of time for hobbies. I think a real man is a person that goes to work and supports his family and do what he can in his neighborhood to help. What a man is supposed to do is take care of his obligations, take care of his family, even if he has to sacrifice himself.

"I never got to see Derek play basketball, and they say he was a better basketball player than he was a football player. I missed all of that working. He was in Hot Springs and broke the Arkansas record of 13.7 in the meter championships. It was a world-class feat, and I missed all of that working. It's rough being a father, especially when you are trying to work so that you can help your kids. It's hard."

Russell attended Horace Mann, a segregated high school, during the late 1950s. His life was profoundly affected by the prevailing social attitudes that incited the subsequent desegregation of Little Rock's public school system. All of his children graduated from Central High School, which remains a symbol of the struggle for justice and equality in education.

"I have a bad flashback when I see people on the street and they say, 'What are you doing here in town? You supposed to be playing pro ball.' So I try to stay away from people because they were always saying that I didn't go as far as I wanted to go. You know, wherever we're going to go, it's all in the Lord's hands. We had our children young, and trying to lead them to go the right way is rough. But I cannot tell them enough how proud I am of them. Everybody said I spoiled my kids, but I think I did the right thing. They all turned out pretty good. I don't think you can do too much for a kid when they're growing up. I don't have a problem because I been a good father. I work and I'm there for them when they need me."

"People say that maybe I was ahead of my time, but I know that God was letting Derek go where I was supposed to go. When I see Derek play, I feel proud and I know that there is some justice."

29

Russell, here with his grandson, encouraged his children to "have dreams and a vision for a better future." His personal sacrifice and commitment helped make those dreams a reality. He doesn't say a lot at family gatherings, but his children feel the strength in his silence.

"I'm proud that I come up as a working man. You can see that by thirty years as a line operator at the Chicopee Textile Factory. All my kids work. I'm proud of that. One thing that me and my wife put into them was to get out and work prior to doing anything else. I got this from my grandfather Henry Russell."

Russell with his daughter Felicia at her college graduation: "Back in the years when I was being raised they didn't really push education a whole lot. That's one thing I hated. That's why me and my wife insisted that our kids were all going to college, because they were not going to make the same mistake I made."

William E. Hickman

Born March 4, 1946, Los Angeles, California

"You remember the small things, like the first time they ride a bicycle or the thrill of them taking to water and learning to swim."

Hickman started his career as a criminal defense and civil rights lawyer. Accomplished in both litigation and corporate finance, he has risen to the position of president and CEO of Avis Capital Group Inc., the investment banking division of Avis Investment Holding Corporation, which maintains offices in the United States and Europe. He and his wife, Althea Robinson, a concert pianist, have twin daughters, Beatrice Jennifer and Angela Rochon.

"When the kids were young we lived down in Palo Alto. I always left my office in the city of San Francisco at five o'clock so that I could have dinner at home. Dinner took one or two hours to eat because we were all talking back and forth to each other. It wasn't a structured conversation, just talking about stuff. dogs, friends at school, how much they hated or loved their tutor . . .

"The twins were both terrific athletes. Angie was second team all-American in Lacrosse, and Jenny was star of her soccer and basketball teams. I didn't have sons, but I ended up treating them both like boys. When they were young we would be outside firing baskets even though the ball was as big as they were. At the same time I enjoyed taking them to ballet and cello lessons, sitting with the other fathers and laughing about the whole experience.

"The twins are always fighting with each other—they hated the word *share*. Every time something would go wrong, Althea and I would call my mother, and she would simply tell us to calm down because 'this too will pass.'"

Hickman's mother, Emily, arrived in California in 1919 when she was two years old. Her father was a physician from Ohio and one of a group of African American professionals who moved to southern California around the turn of the century.

"On my mother's side of the family we are de-scended from a slave named Pleasant Litchford. As the story goes, Pleasant, who was a blacksmith by training, was able to buy his way out of slavery and eventually purchase his mother's freedom. On my father's side, Pascal Hickman, a white man, married Fanny, who was a slave from the Guinea Coast. They had several children, all of whom were set free in the 1830s. We have copies of our freedom papers. It is amazing.

"Although we are fair skinned, we were raised as a proud black family. My father, Richard Hickman, was born in Murfreesboro, Tennessee, in 1917. He went to Fisk and did graduate work at the University of Michigan and Cal-Berkeley. Although his father was a doctor, my father decided to become a health educator. He arrived in California just before World War II and met and married my mother. My parents and grandparents stressed that the privilege of learning was important for our family. I remember as a kid having all these international people over to the house because my father was part of a team that created polio clinics. He was also part of the consulting team to the United Nations on ridding the world of smallpox. He touched many lives and was never down. It was an extraordinarily loving family. I was lucky.

"I loved getting in the car with my father, just riding and having a talk about things. He was a perfect role model for me because he loved my mother so much. My father personified what it means to be a man. He wasn't afraid to show his emotions, to cry at the beauty of the sunset, or to express his joy with his family by tearing up. He was a terrific guy, but he was also a guy you wouldn't want to mess with because he was a strong person.

"My father died when I was a sophomore in high school. There is no way to describe that day. There is no way to get over that. It happens when life is supposed to end. I had him for fourteen years of my life, and I wouldn't trade having that man for fourteen years of my life with any other man for sixty years of my life. I had a terrific childhood. I hope my daughters think of me as I think of my father."

Hickman with his daughter Jenny in Central Park: "Daddy respects me—my mind, my heart, the choices I've made."

Hickman and his daughter Angie: "They are individual human beings with different perspectives on things. You must learn to enjoy being with them and hearing what they have to say."

"One has to spend time with children; that's where it begins. We talked an awful lot as a family, and it helped to keep them grounded. I don't know if there is a secret to anything; it was just being able to spend time and to talk to your children."

Angie with her father in his office: "He'll drop the most important meeting in the world to take time out to talk to us."

Hickman and his daughter Angie with new partners of Avis Capital Group: "A lot of corporate leaders now recognize that it makes economic sense to have blacks, latinos, women in the workforce. They can no longer afford the old-boss network. They have to take a look at the strengths and contributions that all segments of the society bring. The girls and I talk about diversity being one of this country's greatest assets."

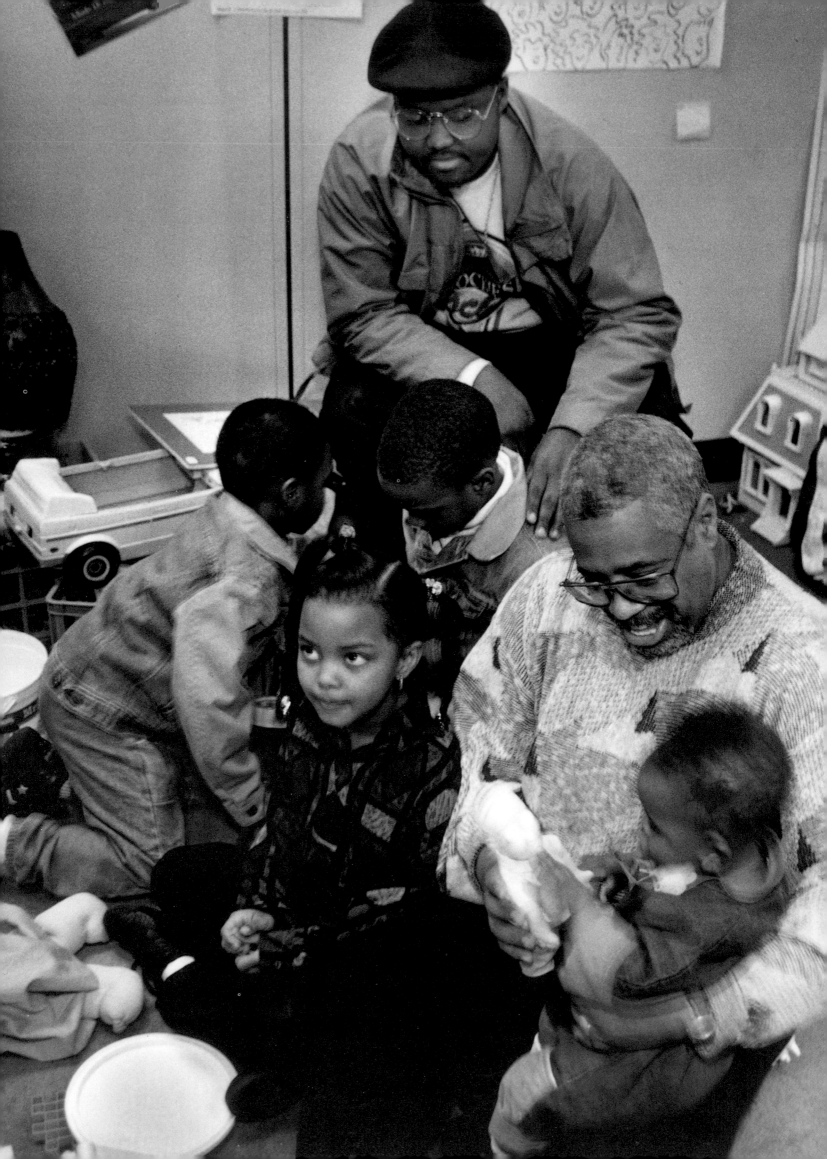

Tom Henry and the Responsive Father's Program

Born April 5, 1946, Cambridge, Maryland

"We talk about their children and how they should teach their children to deal with racism and sexuality. We teach them what an awesome responsibility it is to be a father."

The Responsive Father's Program, under the auspices of the Philadelphia Children's Network, is dedicated to improving the lives of children. Based on a concept defined as father reengagement, the project circumvents the prevailing notion that unmarried fathers are "worthless and dispensable." Developing strategies to encourage and enable fathers to become and remain engaged in caring about and for their children has proved to be a worthy challenge for Tom Henry.

"Recruitment for the Responsive Father's Program was done through churches, community centers, schools, neighborhood centers. But the biggest recruiter was word-of-mouth from young men involved talking to other young men. It was important to access dollars to train these young men so they could get jobs with upward mobility, remain employed, become self-sufficient, and in turn make child-support payments. I use the term *kinetic self esteem* We took the normal stuff—communications, decision making, relationships, and race—and moved it, made it walk from the paper. From the very beginning I knew that this would require a long-term commitment.

"I am a practitioner. I am on the front line, hearing the pain every day and dealing with the problems of these young men. One night a young man came in. He was very upset. He was at a young lady's house that he went to school with because he was showing her some costume jewelry that he was selling. Her boyfriend came in and thought he was there to see her, so he pulled a gun on him. He had his son with him so he was very upset that this guy would pull a gun on him and put his son's life in danger. I said, 'You weighed your options and obviously you made a good decision. You're healthy, your child is healthy, and you're here. Now we must deal with the fact that your ego is hurt.

Somebody pulled a gun on you and threatened you and you couldn't do anything about it.' When I get involved in the life of one of these young men, I don't know where it's going to take me."

Tom and Beverly Henry have been married for thirty-one years. Their commitment to young African American men began nearly twenty-eight years ago in the inner city of Philadelphia with a program named The Do Right. As a young couple with a newborn daughter, they weren't much older than many of the young men they sought to mentor. Nevertheless, they organized basketball and baseball games and helped them get through school and find job opportunities.

"The support group that I run now is called Total Commitment because we must deal with all aspects of a man's life. It must be a holistic approach. I'm proud of the commitment of these young men, particularly those who are not fathers that come faithfully. Some individuals need to have a place to go where they can vent, where they can talk about the lack of employment, inferior schools for their children, the racism, the discrimination they face, and a racist criminal justice system that they must deal with on a daily basis. That's a tremendous load to carry. It's a matter of teaching and educating that there are other ways of dealing with situations than just—to hell with it I'm out of here, or violence.

"My wife and I support this group out of our pockets. There are a lot of people in Philadelphia and around the country who know I'm real about what I do, so they help. I do this because God gave me a mission, and if I don't do it, I'm not doing his will. People ask me how do I continue to do this and work all these long hours. I'm doing God's will, that's what I'm driven by. I don't run to church every Sunday, but I'm a very spiritual person and I pray daily and often. Spirituality must be real. I talk to God every night, and I ask him to give me the strength to go one day at a time and to help somebody. I'll do this until God does not permit me to wake up one morning.

Eric DeLoach of the Responsive Father's Program with his son: "You can't strip away three generations of baggage in six, twelve, or eighteen months. For one to think that they could do that is disrespectful."

"They watch us constantly, every move, twenty-four hours a day. Always be mindful of the kind of role model you need to be."

"What gets left out of the equation is how much these guys care about their children. They think about them. They worry about them."

Shawn Smiley and his daughter: The Responsive Father's Program's goal is to help fathers recognize the costs of parenting, not just in money, but in emotional involvement.

Travis Christian

Born November 29, 1976, Bronx, New York

"I'm always smiling, and anytime you see him he's smiling. I could be mad inside but I'll be smiling. That's something I want him to have. I don't want him to go through life miserable, you know. I don't want him to experience a slight bit of misery, although I know it's going to come sooner or later and that it's part of life."

"I'm not that old, but you can ask anybody and they'll say that Travis has seen and done a lot of stuff. I've seen war because I used to live in one of the worst projects in the Bronx. I've seen people get shot in front of me. I've been shot at. I've seen things you wouldn't believe, but I don't regret it because when you see it, you know it's reality and you don't want to go there.

"I was never really like a street kid. I mean I hung around and everybody knew me and I knew everybody, but I couldn't see myself hanging out on the corner for no apparent reason. I did my share of bad things here and there. I mean everybody has done things you regret, but my mother is a Christian, and I was raised in that totally.

"My little sister's father was around the majority of my childhood. He was the only male in my life from birth to around ten years old. After that, the fatherlike perspective was, 'adios.' There was no one else except my mom. She was always a working woman, you know. She tried to maintain the household a lot most of the time by herself. She had three kids with her. It's not that easy, but she did it. We could have been out there doing God knows what with God knows whom, but she

raised us and we all got good heads on our shoulders."

Christian graduated seventh in his class from Alfred E. Smith High School. His teachers recognized his propensity for mathematics and encouraged him to excel. He currently attends Empire State College and works as an electrical apprentice.

"I've had my ups and downs but I've always been street smart. I've always seen myself as a logically smart person. I've been working consistently since about age sixteen . . . maybe even younger than that. I've always had a job as far as I can remember. I don't know why I'm so busy. Honestly right now in my life I'm where I want to be. I had an opportunity to go to college, but I didn't go. I was going to go to Boston University, but because of my son I stayed. That's the only thing I really regret, but I will not be sad, not one bit. My son is my pride and joy. You can't take him away from me."

On January 28, 1995, Tevor Jeffreal Christian was born to Travis Christian and Stephanie Hunt. Christian is determined that his son will not have an absentee father.

"Tevor is with me every day. His mother works at night, so he stays at my house. The only time he sees his mother is once a week on her day off. I mean it's like a fifty-fifty thing. Most of my friends, when things come along, not going their way, they just leave it alone and take another route. Staying here, sticking it through, and seeing the good and the bad makes you into a man. If you stand there and take the good with the bad it will mold you into something good."

"The birth of my son was the only time in my life I ever cried a tear of joy. It was beautiful. I was full of so many mixed emotions. What was I going to do with a kid when I hadn't totally lived a life yet? I was excited and sad because I was just nineteen."

Roy Cooper Jr.

Born November 3, 1927, Nethersland, Missouri

"An African known as Granny Lett was my Grandpa's great-grandmother. She had children with the man she 'jumped the broom' with, which was a legal marriage ceremony among the slaves. But she also had some children by the master, George Cooper, who had moved to Mississippi from one of the Carolinas. We are their descendants."

"Coming out of slavery, my part of the family was given a section of land in Winston County, near Louisville, Mississippi. As they grew up on the land and people got older, a young white man, who my grandfather said he had known as a kid, put up a rail fence across the better part of the land. When my grandfather asked him what he was doing, he said, 'Alex, this land was given to you boys and this part is just too good for a nigger to have.' Grandfather's brother borrowed money against the undivided part of the land and moved north, but my grandfather stayed. He was determined to find out whether he owned the land or not. It cost $125.00 to have a lawyer check the records, but he worked for two years to come up with the money. Finally, the lawyer came back and told him that the land legally belonged to him but that, at that time, in the state of Mississippi it would take a mighty Christian-hearted white man to give a nigger what he is supposed to have.

It wasn't long before the Night Riders, who were the forerunners to the Ku Klux Klan, started taking black folks' land and running everybody out. So my grandfather left his land with enough equipment to start over and ended up in Arkansas. In 1921, he moved his family to Pemiscot County, Missouri, rented land, and began sharecropping. He had been there for just a short while when one day a sign was put up on the fence post: 'Move out before we kick you out. K.K.K.'

"My grandpa taught me from way back that you deal with each man as an individual. Never let anybody drag you down so low as to make you hate him.

Hate destroys. Nevertheless, he left that land and moved north to a little community they called Swift, Missouri, but he never wanted to own land again."

Roy Cooper Jr. is the oldest of eleven sons and one daughter of the late Roy Cooper Sr. and Louise Black Cooper. The Coopers were sharecroppers until 1939, when they were able to purchase a farm with a loan from the Farmers Home Administration. His parents believed that the sacrifices they made to educate their children would provide an opportunity for them to help others. Six of the Cooper children are graduates of Lincoln University.

"I will never forget the school bus. We had one school bus for the whole school, and it wouldn't come down to pick us up. A group of people got together with my dad and decided to go down to the superintendent and talk to him about it. When it came time to go, nobody showed up. So Daddy went down and talked with the superintendent. As soon as he got back, here they come strolling up. I was standing off in the distance. I wasn't supposed to be hearing this but my dad told them, 'You fellows were supposed to be here this morning. Maybe I shouldn't have gone down there by myself, but let me tell you one thing. I don't need a committee when it comes to my family!' He instilled in us—don't just talk about conditions, find a way to do something about it. I told my kids the same thing."

Roy and Frieda Reagon Cooper have five children, Roy III, Stacy, Tracy, Joe, and Kenny. They represent the third generation to attend Lincoln University. In 1962 Cooper became the first black hired by the Farmers Home Administration in Missouri. Today, he provides government loans to farmers who are struggling to maintain their land.

"To grow up and be a man like my father still delights me. My father was a man of faith. A few days before he passed, he said 'I don't want everybody crying or anything like that. Everything is alright.' Then he told me, 'I want you to pass things on.'"

"I have grandbabies now, and that's the highlight of my life. My little grandboy, I call him 'my main man.' He'll be eight in May and wants to be everything just like papa. He even wants to get a haircut with a bald spot in the middle."

"The man is the responsible being of the household. He is the one that initiates and motivates the things for his family. He is to protect, guide, love, and nurture his wife and family in the fear and admonition of the Lord so that they can be a credit to society. We have subordinated our responsibilities to the schools, churches, teachers, and others. We have accepted mediocrity and let things get out of hand. When you are the man of the house you're supposed to float your own boat."

Cooper taught all his daughters to change tires and understand basic mechanics before they were allowed to drive alone. Stacy explained, "Dad wanted us to be able to take care of ourselves."

Cooper with his son Joe: "I want my kids to remember me as I remember my father. I want them to remember me as one who was considerate to their needs, compassionate, and stern enough on the mistakes that they made. A man that was able to discipline with love. Each child is different, and you have to be a father that will stay close enough to recognize it."

A reunion of family and friends is held each year on the Cooper farm. A collection is taken in support of one lucky student's college costs. Students who have been helped in years past return to report grades, celebrate accomplishments, and give thanks.

Timothy Edward Record

Born March 23, 1970, Los Angeles, California

"I will always be there for my son, because I don't want him to go through what I went through."

"I was born and raised in East L.A., and I grew up too fast. I started to know things too quick. I started out at a young age smoking crack. I smoked it for a good six months, then I got tired of it. I wasn't going to school because I was too busy focusing on getting high. I will never forget one day I went outside, it was my birthday. I was going to turn fifteen years old. I prayed to God and I never smoked crack again. I started 'L.A.ing,' you know, gang-banging in a very known, young, active gang that was pushing heavy drugs. I became the youngest dope dealer in East L.A. I became very strong with the money, you know what I mean? Money bought me anything and everything.

"My mom was still smoking drugs at that time. Everything was so negative—cussing at us, calling us names in front of people. I sucked it in and became real violent and real mean. I became angry because I needed my mom and I didn't have my father. Inside my soul and heart, everybody knew I was a good kid, just growing up in a very nasty world, you know what I mean? You start to explode and to take it out on people. I say to myself, 'I regret a lot of things I did but it's not my fault. I didn't ask for this.' I was involved in the party and all that bull, but I didn't want to live that life. I always wished that somebody would just take me away from here so I wouldn't have to deal with this anymore.

"I never had a father in my life. My mom says my father's been in jail for maybe fifteen years. Well it doesn't give him an excuse. He could have found me, you know what I mean? . . . He could have found me. I will never forget, one day, I was nine years old. It was the first time I ever had a glimpse of this man. He tells me, 'Yeah I'm going to be back tomorrow for Christmas, buy you some Christmas stuff.' I sit there

and waited for that man and he never came. You know what I'm saying? When I see that story on movies I tell people that ain't fake. That's real. Men do that. I will never forget that. I waited man . . . the whole day. So he never came back. I've never seen him again."

Record prayed for an opportunity to break the cycle of violence and crime. He found a way of escape through Father Greg Boyle, a Catholic priest who heads a program entitled Jobs for the Future. Through sheer determination, Record eventually secured a position as office manager of Wendy Finerman Productions, the producers of *Forrest Gump*. With more than five years on the job, he has proved that he is responsible, appreciative, and committed to a positive future.

"All these kids think gang-banging is the way to go. I thought I had respect, acceptance, power. You know what I mean? But it's all bull. A lot of gang members was scared of changes. They ain't going to be loud about it, but they cry when they're in jail. They're moved because they're only that way to get that respect so people don't walk over you. I know for a fact that I cried."

On July 7, 1993, Martha Escalante and Timothy Record became the parents of a son, Andrew Gregory Record. Record strives to ensure that his son will have a life full of resources and opportunities.

"Andrew is my boy. I love him very much. He's a very beautiful kid, you know what I mean? He's very beautiful. He has a strong, strong character. If somebody gets in his face talking crazy, I want him to be strong and say, 'I'm walking away,' you know what I'm saying? 'I'm walking away.' There's no need to be fighting. It takes having a family to give you the strength and encouragement to be somebody. It takes knowing who you are to make it.

"I've got to give him the momentum . . . give him that positive impact that I never got."

"What I love to do with him is read books. He gets into it, and he asks me all these questions, you know what I mean? Why daddy this and that? It's a whole trip being a father. You have to give him love. You got to pay attention to this kid and show him."

"You got to be responsible for your actions. My son is no dummy. He picks up on everything. Whatever you say, whatever you do in front of him, he's going to do it too. It ain't no joke, you got to be careful."

"I pray to God because I want to see my boy grow. I want to see what my father didn't see. I want to be by my son's side. I want to see him do things. I want him to say, 'My dad was my best friend. He was close to me. I could trust my father with anything I said. He was there for me. He gave me advice on how to be a better man.'"

Timothy Pinkney

Born December 6, 1952, Baltimore, Maryland

"Husbands and wives who are pondering divorce must face their problems today, or they're going to face the problems of their children tenfold many years from now. God made us stewards over these children, but we were selfish and didn't take care of those responsibilities when we should have. I could just take the blame and feel sorry for the problems I had earlier in life, but I try not to beat myself up about it. You've just got to go out there, reach out, and do the best you can."

"My mother and father divorced a few years into their marriage, and after that I was raised off and on by both parents until my grandmother, Leanne Pinkney, stepped in to assist my father with raising me. My aunt, Grace Bennett, and her two children were also living with my grandmother, and so the five of us began to live together as one family. As my grandmother grew older, my aunt took me under her wing as one of hers. Wherever she took her girls, she took me too.

"My dad was always in my life. He was a truck driver, and even when he was on the road a far distance away, he would always take time out to call me so that I would be able to talk with him. When he made a promise he always kept it. I look up to him because he always took care of me.

"When I was growing up, I never really threw around a ball with my dad or went to a baseball game. He shared himself by taking me for rides in his truck, and when he had the opportunity he would take me on some of his long-distance trips. I remember one time when I was in college, he redirected his return trip to pick me up. He chained my trunk to the flatbed of his eighteen-wheeler and took me home to Pennsylvania. Those were special times, long hours on the road with him, no music, no TV, just him and I. I wanted to be a truck driver just like him, but out of love he would say, 'Don't do as I do, do as I say because I want you to have an education and a easy life.' He had several bouts with a heart attack, then he got phlebitis, and since the age of forty he has been in so much pain. Even though his health was failing him, he went out there and worked and never complained. He was always a good provider, and I respected him for that."

Pinkney was admittedly self-centered during the early years of his marriage. Pampered by his aunt and grandmother, he was ill-equipped to cope with the responsibilities of fatherhood. He and his wife, Terry, had three children: Vivian, Desiree, and Timothy. With the birth of the third child, "something clicked inside" and he promised to become a more responsible husband; however, it was too late. Their relationship was irreparably damaged, and in 1990 they were divorced after fourteen years of marriage.

"Prior to the divorce I was pretty involved in the kids' daily lives. I took care of the laundry, disciplined the kids, and helped them with their homework. We spent a lot of playful times together, so when the divorce came it was shattering to their lives. I moved to Philadelphia to work, and my wife moved to Maryland. She was having difficulty emotionally trying to raise three children, and her parents asked if I would take my son. Instead of breaking up the children, I decided I would take all of them, and since then I've been a single parent.

"Before the kids came to live with me I was just supporting them monetarily and seeing them on vacations and holidays. When I was just doing that, I knew that they were my children and I was their father, but having a hands-on influence in their lives really makes you feel like you're the dad . . . the father. The daily responsibility of my children brought structure to my life.

"The one thing I never wanted my children to experience has already happened, which is the instability. Presently my son is the only one living with me. He will be with me until he's of age to be on his own. It's hard for the children because they have been going back and forth between mother and father and they are living their lives but they are not stable.

"I am a loving father and I will always be there, which is the most important thing. To me, that's security, a post to lean on. We tried to instill in them that they should respect their elders, trust in family, and always keep their eyes on the Lord, and that it's all right to be honest with your emotions and your feelings. Even though their mother and father are apart, I want them to be proud of who they are and to know that we still love them as a whole . . . together."

Pinkney with his daughter Vivian: "I remember when the scalpel touched my wife's abdomen. I saw the skin just pop open and a few seconds later, I saw the little head come out, and that was Vivian. I would hold her and cherish her all the time, hoping that I wouldn't put her through some of the things that I went through as a child. Little did she know that down the road, daddy was basically going to take her through almost exactly what he went through. It weighs a big scar on me when I see my children go through some of the same problems."

"Children are given to you as a gift from God. They are precious jewels given to us on loan. Anything I have today is because of the grace of God. If my children are alive and well and I'm able to have a job to help me care for them it's not of my doing. It's because of the grace of God."

*"The most important thing as a man is to be a priest . . .
a leader because you should be able to give direction. We're
born innocent and we have a carnal nature, but also there
is a part that is good . . . that is godly. No matter how
much badness you may do, whether a man be Christian,
Muslim, or Hindu, he will always come down to his knees
and look to the heavens when he needs help."*

Pinkney with his son, Timothy: "They came to live with me at the first of January. I didn't like the public schools in our neighborhood. I wanted them to be confident growing up 'round many cultures, so I decided to drive thirty-six miles each way so that they could attend a church school. We had to get up at five-thirty in the morning. It made a long day, but we got the work done."

Thurmon Stubblefield

Born January 18, 1960, Yazoo City, Mississippi

"I want my children to see the real me, the person that I am, and to love me for who I am."

"I feel strongly in my heart that being a man means being a God-fearing person . . . someone that's loving, caring, someone that can give some type of direction to his family, and someone that's hard-working. As far as the physical aspects are concerned, I just wipe that out completely because that ain't being a man. A man is someone that cares for himself, cares about others, and someone that's just a righteous person. A man wants to treat everybody fair but also wants them to treat him fair. He stands up when he's supposed to.

"I look back on growing up in Mississippi as an experience that helped me be stronger. A lot of people take things for granted, like waking up in the morning and going over there and flipping a switch. Well I don't know exactly how old I was, but that didn't happen at my house until maybe I was seven years old. It helps me to appreciate the material things, to appreciate life itself.

"My mother and father were together until I was nine years old, then they separated. Me, my mom, and three brothers came to St. Louis in 1969. My oldest brother, he lived here already, and he came to get us, and we all, like moved into his two-bedroom apartment with his wife and two daughters. My mom had a seventh-grade education and had never worked a job besides in the fields and cleaning somebody's house. Just being able to look back and see where she came from, from nothing and with all those kids, gives me strength even today."

Stubblefield currently works seven days a week and holds four jobs in order to earn enough money to en-sure that his children can live and attend school in a safe environment. He is challenged every day as he endeavors to overcome past problems with substance abuse. He enrolled himself in a rehabilitation program and surrounds himself with the love and support of his wife, Joyce, and their four children: Nikina, Ronnie, Samorie, and Amelia.

"I'm thirty-seven years old and I've experienced a lot of things. I've been out in some areas of St. Louis that normally you couldn't pay me to go, in all times a day and night around folks that I knew nothing about. There was a period when I wasn't home much because I was out doing my thing and I lost a lot of respect from my family. I was going out making money, but hell, I wasn't no place around. I really love my wife because when things kind of started to fall apart, she really held things together for about four years.

"I got a call one Friday night about nine o'clock from my mom. She told me that a young cousin had got shot in the chest, close range with a shotgun over a cassette tape. He was fifteen and really close with my son. Wasted over nothing. This is a complete different generation. They are exposed to a lot of things that we weren't, and the way I look at it, things are a heck of a lot worse. I just don't want to see my children fall into the same mode of thinking because it's too hard and times are changing.

"Sometime I wonder what it would be like if I just load them all up in the van and just take them around and show them some places, so they would actually know what I've been through. I would hate for them to think that their daddy's the best daddy and he ain't never did no wrong. I turned my life over to God. I can't handle it by myself because I know I'm weak in certain areas. It ain't about not being a man because it takes strength to admit you're weak."

Stubblefield with his daughter Amelia: "Having my baby daughter made me open my eyes and say that I can't be any good to her whatsoever if I continued to live the way I'd been living. Then I lost my job the week after she was born. That was a rough blow. I've never been a lazy person. I had spent thirteen years of my life working on my job and a lot of the people were pretty much like family. I put in a lot of hours but I was hurt when they let me go and it took me awhile to stop worrying about it."

"I don't want a family like the Partridge family or anything like that. I just want a very close-knit family. I just want to live a comfortable life. I don't want to be rich, I just want to know that my family is taken care of. I don't want to be able to give my kids everything, but I do want to be able to provide for them and I want them to grow up to be responsible."

Stubblefield with his daughter Samorie: "I'm trying to work on bringing us back together as a family. I had to come to grips with myself on the fact that we don't build relationships overnight. It goes back to trust, you just have to learn to trust each other. There are still some rough turns on the right path, but I just ask God to give me strength."

Clyde Ruffin

Born October 21, 1952, Kansas City, Missouri

"I prayed daily for the same closeness with my children that I had experienced with my own mother and for the strength to be the provider that I perceived my father to be. From the very beginning my role as father seemed to revolve around my ability to provide for my family and protect them. I wanted my children to trust me and to know that I would never abandon them."

"My father was born into a family that owned nothing. There was no family history or traditions. They were uneducated, dirt-poor, living in the backwoods of Louisiana when he and my mother met and were married. He has a vivid memory of a fight between his parents that happened when he around three years old. My grandfather, who was an alcoholic, attempted to kill his wife by stabbing her several times. My father has never completely resolved the emotional turmoil from witnessing this attack on his mother. When I was growing up, my father was never affectionate. There were no hugs, pats on the head, or arm around the shoulder. No wrestling matches on the floor. But when I touch the rough skin of his hands and feel the stiffness of his strong fingers, I understand how hard he has worked for us. We were not well-off, but somehow we were always provided for.

"The miracle is that even during the difficult times, when my father was fighting his personal demons, I believed that I could look in his eyes and tell how he felt about us. His love has been like a powerful river that runs underground. Regardless of what was happening in our family, I have always been confident that he would surrender his life for mine."

Ruffin met his wife, Sheila, while attending the University of Iowa in the early 1970s. Many young people, disenchanted with the civil rights movement, were beginning to embrace the ideology of black nationalism. Ruffin's involvement with the black arts movement during this period nurtured his creativity and solidified his interest in the African American experience. He and his wife try to share that experience with their four daughters, Mikisha, Joi, Candace, and Jessica.

"It was always 'Clyde and his girls' because it was obvious how I felt about those children. When they were babies I touched and held them often. We played house, danced in the living room, and watched the sunset. But now that they are young women, the play has turned into midnight conversations about life, boys, school, and the future. Even though I miss my baby girls, these are the best of times.

"There are days when my greatest fear is that something will happen to one of them and that there will be absolutely nothing I can do about it. I have learned that I can't protect them against their will. Sometimes they put themselves in compromising positions that are beyond your protection. We are working every day on building the trust, but at some point you have to release them and believe that you have planted 'commonsense' seeds.

"My obligation is to not retreat but to press in. To not stand by in silence but to speak my mind, to say what I think—what I expect, to tell them when I think they are wrong and to try to do whatever I can in their behalf. I believe that the challenge is to find the line between giving them roots—a sense of place and belonging, a sense of family, of security—and giving them wings. I have decided that they must learn to fly. They will make mistakes and if they want to be caught, they will let me know."

Ruffin with Candace and Jessica: "I have an eternal bond with my children. They will always be my daughters, and I will be their father. If they will remember me as 'Papa,' a man who gave of himself, I will be satisfied that it has been worth the struggle."

Ruffin with Jessica: "I have always designed clothes and made all kinds of unique things for them because, for me, it was an act of love."

"I want them to have an appreciation of family, history, culture, and to be proud of their 'blackness.' I want them to be able to withstand the sting of racism. When they were young, I would ask elderly relatives and friends to hold them and give them their blessing because I believed that there could be a profound spiritual exchange in their embrace."

"My mother's grandmother, Charity Phillips, inherited forty acres of land in Mooringsport, Louisiana, that had been purchased by her father in the 1870s. She was a woman with a keen vision of the future and was able to increase the landholdings to a hundred and twenty acres. My relatives still live on her land. My maternal grandmother, Mary Liza, died in 1930, at the age of forty-one, of complications from asthma following the birth of her fourteenth child. My mother was only four years old at the time, but she is a resilient woman. I hope that my children will inherit this legacy of strength and independence."

Kwanza celebration: "The most important thing
in life is to replenish the earth with decent, caring,
loving human beings."

About the Contributors

Carole Patterson is a photographer whose work has been featured in more than forty solo exhibitions from coast to coast, including shows in Los Angeles, New York, and Mexico City. Her three-year touring exhibition *Capturing the Spirit: Portraits of Contemporary Mexican Artists* was organized and toured by the Smithsonian Institution Traveling Exhibition Service (SITES).

Anthony Barboza is a highly regarded New York photographer whose work has been featured in *Songs of My People* and *Black Culture and Modernism*. His work is included in the permanent collection of the Museum of Modern Art, New York City; the Studio Museum of Harlem, New York; and the University of Ghana, Africa.

Arvarh Strickland, Emeritus Professor of History at the University of Missouri–Columbia, is the author or editor of several books. His most recent book is *Selling Black History for Carter G. Woodson: A Diary, 1930–1933, by Lorenzo J. Greene.*

Minion KC Morrison is Professor of Political Science at the University of Missouri–Columbia. He has written three books and numerous articles on African and African American politics and civilization.

Clyde Ruffin is the founding director of the University of Missouri's award-winning Black Theatre Workshop and has worked professionally as a director, designer, and actor. He has won numerous awards as a teacher and served as Chair of the Department of Theatre at the University of Missouri from 1990 to 1995.

Marlene Perchinske is Director of the Museum of Art and Archaeology, University of Missouri–Columbia. Prior to her current position, she exhibited her art internationally and worked for the Museum of Modern Art in New York City for sixteen years.